GLORY
DAYS

RT

The History of a Classic London Bus

Kevin McCormack

IAN ALLAN
Publishing

Front cover:
Route 122 was one of four services to lose their RT allocations on 22 April 1978. Plumstead's RT1755 stands at Crystal Palace on 19 February 1977.
Ernie Sargieson

Back cover:
The withdrawal of the London RT from passenger service made 1979 a bleak year for bus enthusiasts, but the emergence of the former mobile instruction unit No 1037J as the newly-restored RT1 brought some welcome cheer. In a recreation of its pre-service appearance in spring 1939, RT1 looks magnificent as it passes through Islington while taking part in the anniversary Bus Parade on 8 July 1979. *Geoff Rixon*

Title page:
RT4211 takes an early bath in the River Brent on its way to Chiswick Swimming Pools. Such was the state of Ruislip Road East on 4 December 1960. *Mike Pope*

CONTENTS

First published 1998

ISBN 0 7110 2581 9

Published by Ian Allan Publishing

an imprint of Ian Allan Ltd, Terminal House, Station Approach, Shepperton, Surrey TW17 8AS.
Printed by Ian Allan Printing Ltd at its works at Coombelands in Runnymede, England.

Code: 9804/B3

INTRODUCTION

There have been a great many books on London buses over the last few years, including several dedicated to the famous Routemaster (RM). However, its distinguished predecessor, the RT-type, has been largely overshadowed and so, with the 60th anniversary of its introduction and the 20th anniversary of its withdrawal from regular service occurring in 1999, I hope to redress the balance a little with this title, recalling the glory days of the RT.

Buses of the RT family dominated London's Central and Country areas during the 1950s and 1960s, and, through a remarkable series of 'Houdini' acts, survived virtually until the end of the 1970s. Not that the RT was confined to London: in addition to a few new RTs delivered to provincial operators, large numbers of secondhand vehicles gave sterling service throughout Britain and around the world. Indeed, a few continue to do so today, in places as diverse as Guernsey, South Africa, Canada and the USA. But you won't find them in regular service in their rightful place, London, apart from one on the southern boundary of the former Country Area at East Grinstead.

The RT story started in 1938 when a new revolutionary AEC running unit, disguised by an old outside-staircase body, was tested in passenger service for six months. Meanwhile, at Chiswick Works, a modern, sleek body was being constructed. The two parts were joined together in spring 1939 and RT1 was born. In the summer, RT1 hit the national headlines as it made its public début, but the excitement it generated was shortlived. Within weeks, World War 2 was declared and RT1 joined the remainder of the London Transport (LT) fleet in serving Londoners during the dangerous times ahead. Between January 1940 and January 1942, a further 150 RTs entered service before wartime restrictions brought an end to production.

Lessons learnt from the first RTs, coupled with technological advances, resulted in the production of the postwar RT and its Leyland counterparts, the RTL and the 8ft-wide RTW. By the time production ended in 1954, an incredible 6,956 members of the RT family had been built

for London, not to mention 15 float (spare) bodies and 41 provincial LT-style RTs.

LT had at last achieved its goal of having a bus fleet with as few vehicle types as possible – indeed, this was the largest fleet of standardised buses anywhere in the world. Following the withdrawal of the postwar STLs on 31 May 1955, the only double-deck buses in passenger service in London were vehicles of the RT family, with the exception of 76 lowbridge RLHs. In reality, the RT-type's monopoly lasted only eight months, broken by the prototype Routemaster which entered service in February 1956. Nevertheless, the RT family would have nothing to fear from the RM until the mid-1960s; instead, a different problem faced the RT – too many had been built. The reduction in passenger journeys in the mid-1950s as a result of increasing car ownership and home entertainment – television replacing the cinema, for example – had not been anticipated. Consequently, the entire RT fleet was never in service simultaneously, although, in its peak year of operation (1954), the class was only some 200 short of its potential maximum. In fact, some of the last RTs (built in 1954) did not actually enter service until 1959, by which time they were replacing earlier versions of the type! It is remarkable that, as far as its revenue-earning career in London is concerned, the RT class entered service over a period of 20 years and was withdrawn over a period of 24 years.

By the time the RMs dispatched the last trolleybuses to the scrapyard in 1962, the writing was on the wall – or meant to be – for the RT class. Intended for a working life of 15 years, many of those still running had reached this target. But then fate intervened. Although the arrival of further RMs enabled the Leyland versions – the RTL and RTW – and the earliest postwar roofbox-fitted RTs to be withdrawn, RM deliveries ceased in 1968, leaving over 3,600 RTs still to be replaced. Service cuts would help reduce the figure, but the brave new world of One-Person Operation had now dawned and LT ordered vast quantities of new single- and double-deck buses for the Central and Country areas. Their arrival would quickly eliminate the RT, according to the pundits. However, no one anticipated the

This congested scene in Lewisham High Street was taken at the beginning of July 1952, during the last tram week. The principal players are RTL188 and 'HR/2' tram No 1858, which surprisingly carries an accurate chalked inscription. This lucky veteran escaped to Chessington Zoo and is now displayed at Carlton Colville. *Author's Collection*

unreliability of the new buses or the shortage of RM spares which were to bedevil LT and its Country Area successor, London Country. The RT-type's great escape had begun.

London Country, having inherited 484 green RTs on 1 January 1970, was desperate to phase out the class, together with their conductors, but still found it necessary to overhaul a significant number in 1971/2 with five-year 'tickets'. This proved a wise strategy, providing essential cover for ailing modern vehicles. Indeed, despite serviceability improving in 1977, London Country decided to take no chances and recertified the four best RTs, the last of which remained in passenger service until September 1978.

Meanwhile, LT had been confident of getting rid of its passenger-carrying RTs by 1975, but ended up by buying back 34 from London Country as well as embarking on a limited recertification programme. Facing a similar serviceability crisis to London Country in 1976/7, LT was forced to employ RTs on routes on which they had not operated for years, or never operated before, much to the delight of enthusiasts. To add insult to injury, in 1978 LT was reduced to borrowing privately-owned RTs and RTLs

for learner duties because of a shortage of training buses. Nevertheless, this was definitely to be the RT-type's last year in public service – until a narrow bridge at Chadwell Heath upset the plans. A final reprieve of six months, until 7 April 1979, ensured that the RT class reached its 40th year of passenger service.

For a whole generation of enthusiasts who had grown up with RTs and watched them dodge withdrawal for so long, the total elimination of these machines from the streets of London still came as a shock. A handful continued for a short time as trainers for both LT and London Country, the last of all being the Chiswick skid bus, but the RM quickly snatched the mantle of the archetypal London bus and consigned the RT to oblivion. Even the RT-type's record of 40 years' passenger service has been beaten by the RM, which has now clocked up over 42 years. The last RTs in service were between 25 and 31 years old, a seemingly unchallengeable record, yet all the short RMs still running in London are between 34 and 39 years old and, with new engines in the London examples, are destined to last for at least a few more years. But this does not mean that the RM is necessarily a better or more successful bus than the RT – it is more a case of the RM being the last of the line, a type whose demise would mean the end of a tradition which, according to current public opinion, should be cherished.

After the desolate years of the early 1980s, a minor renaissance in RT operation occurred when two independent operators, Ensignbus and Blue Triangle, renovated a handful of the type and put them into limited service. This work included occasional forays on to the No 62, the type's last route which by now had been put out to tender. In the 1990s, with the increasing popularity of heritage services, several ex-London buses are in regular summer service, but you are still more likely to find yourself travelling on a member of one of the smaller classes, the GS for example, rather than on an RT, unless you visit the Bluebell Railway. If only there was an RT operation comparable to Reading Mainline's expanding Routemaster empire. There are, of course, many vehicles of the RT family in preservation, but there seem to be fewer around than in the 1970s, probably because at that time they were acquired in running order. Keeping them going over the years with shortage of finance and accommodation problems is a different matter, however. Other members of the RT family can be found dotted around the world, by now often derelict or serving as burger bars. It would be wonderful, though, if some of the forgotten RTs, RTLs and RTWs emerged for the 1999 celebrations.

There is no doubt that the RT family has an enormous following among bus enthusiasts. Many, like me, may have initially resented their arrival in London because they were so numerous, they all looked virtually the same and they killed-off the great variety of earlier types. It seemed that they would last for ever, so we took them for granted. But the phasing out of the Leyland models and the roofbox RTs changed this perception. Who could fail to admire this maid of all work and bastion of reliability as it survived, usually in unkempt condition, through the 1970s, saving the day for LT and London Country as these operators struggled to keep later generations of buses on the road? Indeed, many of these lumbering hulks reached the scrapyard before the last RTs, after less than 10 years' service.

Admirers of the RT family will all have their own special memories, as I do. Brought up near Ealing Broadway in the postwar years, surrounded by red RTs, I had to make do, for variety, with the rumbling RTLs on the No 112 route. I was just too young to know about Ian Allan bus spotting books when 10 green RTs ran for three months on the No 97 in late 1953. I became a spotter about a year later and will never forget recording my first green RT, dragging my long-suffering mother from the opposite side of Ruislip Lido to note down the number (RT1001). Another vivid memory was taking a torch out into what was probably the last London smog and saving a disorientated No 97 bus from entering someone's front garden at the junction of Woodfield Road and Mount Avenue. Bliss occurred in 1973 when, upon marriage, I moved to High Street, Harlington, where I could watch RTs on the No 140 pass my living room window and speculate how long they would last (ironically, one week after I moved to Surrey in 1978). But my passion for the RT family was truly cemented when I

was persuaded by an office colleague to join the Double Decker Club of Twickenham in 1967 and follow in the footsteps of Cliff Richard. Lots of fun ensued on these outings, such as travelling the length of France perched on the bonnet of RTL1023 and pushing RTL1050 up Reigate Hill! Happily, this last-mentioned bus is in fine fettle today, even though the signatures of the Beatles on the inside of the upper-deck roof – the bus was used in the film *A Hard Day's Night*, but the scene was cut – have long since disappeared (as did the whole roof later, until the present owner acquired a replacement).

It has been a great source of enjoyment to compile this book and to learn facts about the RT of which I was unfamiliar or which I had forgotten. My only problem has been narrowing down the selection of pictures and having to omit so much good material. My thanks go to all the photographers who have contributed: Geoff Rixon, to whom particular credit must go for his early black and white views and who assisted me considerably, Dave Brown, C. Carter, Dave Edwards, Michael Fennell, Roy Hobbs, Mike Lloyd, John May, Gerald Mead, Trevor Muir, Peter Plummer, Mike Pope, Fred Richards and the late Mike Harries of Dorking, whose excellent transparencies have featured in other books that I have compiled and who sadly died suddenly in January 1997. For research I have relied on the 'Bible' which unfortunately is now out of print and has become a collector's item. I am referring, of course, to Ken Blacker's book entitled *RT – The Story of a London Bus*, published by Capital Transport in 1979. Finally, I must thank Bill Ballard, Mike Burgess, Malcolm King, Graham Lunn, Ian McGregor and David Thrower for their invaluable help; also my daughter, Amber, for helping me proof read.

In writing this title – *Glory Days: RT* – I hope to have captured something of the spirit of the vehicles belonging to the RT family and rekindled memories of this wonderful type.

Kevin R. McCormack
Ashtead, Surrey
September 1997

The Prewar RT

The RT family of London buses was synonymous with standardisation on a massive scale, the seeds of which had been sown many years before the first RT was to appear. The main predecessor company of the London Passenger Transport Board – the London General Omnibus Co – saw the benefits of standardisation when it developed the famous B-type bus before World War 1. The LGOC then went on to centralise vehicle repair, previously undertaken by individual garages, by building Chiswick Works in 1924, where design and bodywork manufacture were also undertaken. The STL bus was intended to be the LGOC's new standard class, and the first entered service just before the newly-formed LPTB assumed control of London's buses on 1 July 1933.

The STL class consisted of 2,701 vehicles, but although they were all AEC Regents, there were many variants, particularly with regard to bodywork. LT therefore decided to start again and design the ultimate standard bus. Based once more on the AEC Regent chassis, but radically updated, the new bus would benefit from lessons learnt from the STL and the superior, more powerful, Leyland STD. The key was to have a large engine de-rated, producing greater economy and reducing wear and tear. In addition, the running unit would offer powerful acceleration, smooth braking, easy gear changes and automatic chassis lubrication. Given that the speed of traffic was largely dependent on the bus, this new Regent would keep London moving and also take much of the hard work out of driving.

The origins of the RT acronym are unclear. 'Regent Three' or 'Regent Type' have been suggested, but as the chassis was not known as the Regent Three until the early 1940s and STs and STLs were all Regents, perhaps 'RT' simply stood for 'R Type'. Anyhow, RT1's chassis was

◀◀ The aluminium stripes, curve to the cab door and push-out ventilator above the windscreen are clues to RT19's body having come from RT1. Two years after its last overhaul in spring 1951, RT19 looks past its prime as it lays over at Cromwell Road, Kingston, next to the rear entrance of the bus garage. *Geoff Rixon*

◀ RT2, one of the prewar examples to lose its offside rear indicator just after the war, stands on the cobbles at York Way, alongside King's Cross station. This bus was subsequently sold to the A1 Service consortium of Ardrossan, Scotland. *Geoff Rixon*

completed at Southall in June 1938 and since the body, which was being constructed at Chiswick, was far from ready and the running unit needed to be tested in service, the latter was disguised by the fitting of a Dodson 56-seat body of antiquated appearance complete with outside staircase. This body, built in 1932, had originally been mounted on a Leyland chassis which had worked for the City Motor Omnibus Co, until it had been taken over by LT and numbered TD111. The new hybrid was designated ST1140 and licensed for service on 13 July 1938, moving round the corner to Hanwell – later renamed Southall – garage. After just under six months' service, ST1140 was withdrawn on 31 December 1938 and the body scrapped in April 1939.

In the same month, RT1's proper body was ready and it is fair to say that it caused a sensation, being quite different from anything seen before. Unlike other double-deckers built at Chiswick, which were timber-framed, RT1 was metal-framed; it was the first LT bus to have an all-enclosed cab – only trolleybuses had doors at this time – and it had a bright and cheerful interior. The design of the bus followed contemporary streamlined practice, with rounded corners, and its front nearside wing swept up to the bulkhead (as previously pioneered on an STL). Roof number boxes were fitted to the front and rear domes and the body was decorated with bands of polished, ribbed aluminium (although these were painted over before the vehicle entered service). It was undoubtedly a beautiful vehicle.

RT1 was shown off to the public on 13 July 1939 wearing a set of blinds for Sutton garage, although it never operated from there. It entered service on 9 August 1939 at Chelverton Road, Putney, and this garage and neighbouring Putney Bridge were to receive the first production vehicles.

The RT2-type, as the production vehicles were designated, differed from RT1 in various minor visual respects, such as the shape of the window in the cab door and absence of features such as the swept back mudguards, push-out ventilator above the windscreen, offside staircase window and aluminium strips. But there was a more fundamental, albeit concealed, difference, which ultimately accounted for RT1's body outliving the RT2s' by 15 years:

the RT2 bodies were wooden-framed. In addition, these bodies were not self-supporting at the platform end. However, this made the RT2-type lighter and thus able to carry 56 passengers as opposed to RT1, which was restricted to 55 passengers to keep within the weight restrictions applicable at that time. Nevertheless, it was a retrograde step to revert to wooden framing because of the tendency of these bodies to sag in later life, but LT had no other choice. A total of 338 chassis were ordered, in batches of 150 and 188 (plus three float bodies), and Chiswick was simply not equipped to mass produce metal-framed bodies.

The RT2s are popularly known as 'prewar RTs', but this is something of a misnomer because, although the vehicles were ordered in 1938, war had begun before the first two, RT15 and RT23, were delivered on 13 October 1939. In fact, it was not until 2 January 1940 that the first members entered service on route Nos 28, 30, 37 and 72, whilst the last of the batch, RT151, did not appear until 1 February 1942. Wartime restrictions prevented the second batch from being built.

The new buses proved popular except in one rather important respect: poor braking. The novel air-braking system had to be modified, but parts were hard to obtain. The problem became so serious that most of the fleet were withdrawn on 1 August 1940 and some even suffered the indignity of serving for a time as mess rooms for the Home Guard. Gradually, they re-entered service, but it was not until later in the war that the braking system was fully satisfactory. An inauspicious start, some may say, for this much heralded wonder bus, but it must be remembered that, ironically, this was a small class of non-standard vehicles having to prove itself under the most difficult circumstances. Taking everything into account, the RT2s acquitted themselves well.

The RT had been costly to develop and, during the early 'phoney war' period before the bombing started, AEC was hoping to secure some provincial orders. One bus had already been sold to Glasgow Corporation, based on the RT chassis but with a provincial Weymann body. So it was that RT19 was selected to become a demonstrator. The bus set off on its travels in February 1940, not returning until

August 1942 – unfortunately with an empty order book. By this time there was a real war on and life was very different; bus building would be largely limited to wartime austerity designs and Chiswick's manufacturing capacity would be switched to aircraft production.

The 151 RTs survived the war with none totally written off. The worst casualty was RT66, whose body was destroyed. RTs Nos 59 and 97 were badly damaged and were repaired by Birmingham City Transport, although RT97 did ▶▶ not re-enter service at that stage. RT110 lost its front roofbox and unwittingly brought about the demise of the roofbox altogether, following subsequent trials. Yet, even before hostilities ceased in Europe in May 1945, LT was planning an updated postwar RT, with all-metal body similar to RT1, as well as a revised chassis design. It was not possible to build a new chassis at this stage and so RT19's somewhat under-used chassis was chosen for modification to be the prototype for the postwar RT when manufacture

was permitted. RT19's body was removed in March 1945 and, through various exchanges, was indirectly used to replace RT66's body. On 18 August 1945, RT1 was withdrawn and its metal body, which was compatible with the redesigned RT2-type chassis, was placed on RT19. The painted-over aluminium strips survived, as did the other unique features except for the staircase offside window and the single seat, the body reverting to a 56-seater following a relaxation in weight limits. The hybrid RT19 re-entered service in November 1945 and RT1's original chassis was broken up for spares in September 1946.

In addition to RT19, another RT was undergoing changes, this time the repaired RT97. LT ran a 'Pay As You Board' experiment between 1944 and 1946, initially using two trolleybuses and two STLs. The idea was to eliminate fare dodging and give conductors an easier life. Seats were removed to create a large platform area, and doors fitted. The conductor sat by a cash machine and passengers would congregate on the platform and pay as the vehicle travelled along. RT97 was chosen to demonstrate a rear entrance/exit layout. This necessitated major rear-end modifications, including repositioning of the staircase. The vehicle entered service on 2 January 1946 from Kingston garage where it was used on route No 65. As the bus consistently ran late because there were frequently too many passengers to fit on the platform with the doors closed, the experiment was abandoned and RT97 was taken off the road on 25 March 1946.

'Pay As You Board' had not yet been tried on the less densely used Country services and so RT97 was repainted into Green Line livery and sent to Romford, where it started work on route No 721 on 18 April 1946. Boarding delays still occurred, however, and so on 2 July 1946 the experiment ended. Nevertheless, RT97 had proved popular in other respects and so it remained at Romford until 5 January 1947 operating conventionally. It then returned to Chiswick to undergo a complete metamorphosis.

When RT97 re-entered service on 6 April 1949, it was as a new Green Line coach prototype, RTC1. Apart from the rear roof dome and emergency exit, the vehicle bore no resemblance to an RT. The radiator was relocated below the staircase and a sloping bonnet and grille fitted. The interior modifications included air conditioning and fluorescent lighting. RTC1 represented a bold attempt at creating a modern double-deck coach, but it failed to live up to its promise. Problems with overheating and complaints about its soft suspension brought about its relegation to ordinary bus work in December 1949 spending its remaining years at Leatherhead before withdrawal in March 1953.

Surprisingly, despite being partially stripped, a buyer was eventually found and RTC1 started a new career with Vernons, the football pools company, as a staff bus, where it lasted for several years before being scrapped.

The early postwar years were largely uneventful for the remainder of the prewar RTs. The class stayed intact apart from RT85, which burnt out on route No 74 on 14 May 1949, and RT22, which overturned on 2 January 1951 while working on route No 93 and was damaged beyond repair. RT1's body was removed from RT19 and fitted to the ex-STL chassis of SRT45 in October 1954, becoming mobile instruction unit No 1019J in the service fleet. A more modern chassis became available for the body when a postwar Cravens-bodied vehicle, RT1420, hit a low bridge and in June 1956, RT1, by now in its final form, was renumbered 1037J. Unused by the late 1970s and stored at the back of West Ham garage, this amazing survivor was sold for preservation in the autumn of 1978, making a spectacular début at the head of the procession of last RTs on 7 April 1979. Although it is quite extraordinary that LT decided not to preserve the vehicle itself, someone must have been looking after its interests over the years, ensuring that the body was transferred to a succession of different chassis.

When the year 1955 dawned, 146 of the 150 RT2s remained in stock, of which 129 were still in passenger service. This was meant, however, to be their last year, but seven earned a reprieve due to a weak bridge at Broxbourne in Hertfordshire. Country Area route No 327 was operated by postwar non-standard STLs, which were sufficiently new to fetch a good secondhand price. The bridge was due for strengthening anyway and so it made sense to replace the STLs with the best of the remaining RT2s, the postwar

type being too heavy. Thus, as the Central Area RT2s were withdrawn on 31 May 1955, so the lucky seven – Nos 36, 62, 79, 93, 114, 128 and 137 – became the first members of the class to wear green and re-entered service at Hertford on the following day. With red RT133 retained as a spare, these RTs ran until 1 September 1957, whereupon they joined their contemporaries on training duties.

Although the RT2s were still mechanically sound, their wooden-framed bodies were showing their age. Seventeen of the worst vehicles were disposed of in December 1955, constituting the first RT sales. The remainder became staff or training buses, but redundant RTLs took over as staff buses by November 1958. The displaced RT2s were then used to replace the worst trainers. The last RT2 on training duties, green RT79, was withdrawn on 13 February 1963, leaving one survivor, RT106, which, as No 1036TV in the service fleet, was used in the ignominious role of a practice turnover vehicle for breakdown crews. The vehicle lasted until 1971, when it was sold for spares. Two other RT2s are worth mentioning for their after-life: RT73 achieved fame by touring Russia at the height of the Cold War in August 1959, showing there was life still in these old warriors, and the chassis of RT74 was loaned to the Metropolitan Police College for training in February 1960, returning to LT in September 1968 before being sold for spares.

For a pioneering class, the prewar RT served LT well and some continued in passenger service with other operators or in miscellaneous commercial use well into the 1960s. Five – Nos 8, 44, 54, 113 and 141 – are believed to survive in preservation.

The Standard Postwar RT

In the later stages of the war, a sense of victory and subsequent peace began to be felt in Britain and LT turned its thoughts once more to the continuation of its standardisation policy and the resumption of RT construction. In April 1944, AEC signed up with LT to produce an initial 1,000 RT chassis as soon as circumstances would allow. LT originally intended to build the bodies at Chiswick, but abandoned this idea because of

the volume of overhaul and repair work necessary on the existing bus fleet. Approaches were made to two outside contractors who had previously built metal-framed bodies for LT: Park Royal (of Park Royal, London NW10) and Weymann (of Addlestone, Surrey). Agreement was reached for each to make 250 bodies.

The postwar RT was not greatly different in appearance from the prewar version, although it had more in common with the prototype RT1 than the production RT2s because the body was metal-framed with a self-supporting rear section. A more powerful engine was fitted due to the vehicles being heavier, but the basic dimensions were the same since legal restrictions had yet to be relaxed. The rear roofbox was abandoned as this had fallen into disuse and, following experiments with RT110, a decision was also taken to dispense with the front roofbox. However, this decision was too late to prevent the first batches of the postwar RTs having roofboxes. The nearside route stencil was no longer required because the number would be included in the blind display above the platform. A similar

◀◀ Entering service in May 1948 at Seven Kings garage, Weymann-bodied RT542 had been transferred to Putney Bridge when photographed on 14 March 1953 at Oxford Road, Putney. *Geoff Rixon*

▲ RT4423, seen here at Ponders End, belongs to the batch which carried ex-SRT bodies. The unfortunate abbreviation for 'garage' is reminiscent of London Country in the 1970s. *Geoff Rixon*

decision had been taken over the offside route stencil, but this was quickly reversed, again too late, however, for the earliest postwar RTs and some of the prewar RTs then being overhauled, which had them fitted/refitted later. But perhaps the most obvious external difference between the two types was the design of the lower edge of the cab windows, which was now horizontal. The greatest change, however, was the use of jigs throughout the body manufacturing process, which ensured that identical components were produced and thus guaranteed full interchangeability. Very close tolerances were also required for the chassis. Naturally, Park Royal and Weymann had to construct identical bodies, all with interchangeable components. Apart from the builders' plates by the staircase, the only way of distinguishing the bodies was to examine the bottom left-hand corner of the windscreen from the outside. If the moulding below the driver's offside window continued to the windscreen rubber, then it was a Park Royal body; if it stopped short in line with the moulding below the windscreen, then it was a Weymann body. This was a reliable test only when the bodies were new because in later life the moulding could be altered on overhaul or repair.

The new buses, designated the RT3-type, were delivered in the standard postwar livery with cream upper-deck window surrounds, but retaining the wartime reduced blind displays introduced in order to save linen. The first vehicles also carried the large white disc to the left of the rear numberplate; this had been applied to all buses, but not trolleybuses, as a signal to trolleybus drivers in the blackout that they could overtake the vehicle ahead.

AEC was able to keep reasonably close to chassis delivery timescales, starting from March 1946. Unfortunately, shortages of body materials and skilled labour, coupled with the need to manufacture special tools and jigs, delayed the production of bodies and eventually would have far-reaching consequences. In fact, AEC sold its first RT chassis to provincial operators, but since they did not receive LT-style bodies they bore little external resemblance to RTs apart from the radiator. The first postwar LT RT arrived at Chiswick Works on 28 April 1947:

A group of RTs, which includes Nos 787, 771, 2817 and 2162, congregates in Hounslow garage. Weymann-bodied RT2162 still carries the red and cream livery applied by the body manufacturer until April 1950. *Geoff Rixon*

Swaps between the Central and Country areas were not uncommon in the early 1950s. In the top photograph, taken at Dorking, red RT226 copes with an old blind intended for use with a wartime restricted display. Below, the dreary surroundings of Hertford bus station seem in keeping with the battered appearance of red RT2674. *Geoff Rixon (both)*

This view taken at Kingston station features green RT638 alongside RT2635 and T719, both in red livery. *Geoff Rixon*

RT402 from Weymann. This was followed on 12 May by Park Royal's first, RT152. RT402 entered service on 10 May 1947 from Leyton garage, working alongside open-staircase LTs on route No 10. The contrast between these vehicles could not have been greater and put into perspective the antiquity of many of London's buses and the urgent need to replace them. A new era had dawned.

Further orders were placed with Park Royal and Weymann, adding to the original 500 bodies. The next 250, all RTs except for the prototype Leyland (RTL501), still carried the outdated front roofbox, but the last 150 of these bodies were slightly different. Later designated RT10s, the most noticeable distinguishing feature was the raised front canopy, resulting in the cream central waist band running virtually along the top edge. Another feature, which followed the construction of RTL501, was that the lower line of the cab front was upswept rather than horizontal in order to clear the square dumb iron of the Leyland chassis. This alteration was necessary to achieve interchangeability between RT and RTL bodies.

Park Royal and Weymann now found themselves in a position to manufacture the body which LT had wanted all along: no front roofbox and incorporating the resulting revised front blind display. In addition, a new canopy roof number-box was fixed to replace the previous pillar-mounted stencil number. These changes were introduced on Park Royal's 451st body and Weymann's 301st; these corresponded with RT852 and RT1012 respectively. Park Royal was contracted to build the greater proportion of bodies by virtue of being the larger company. The first non-roofbox RTs entered service in October 1948.

Park Royal and Weymann continued to produce vast quantities of RT and RTL bodies over the next few years, with no visible material alterations apart from the loss of cream around the upper deck windows. The new all-red/all-green livery (apart from the cream central waist band) was introduced in March/April 1950 and started with Park Royal's RT1678 and Weymann's RT3115. This change arose from LT's proposed introduction of spray painting and the need for a simplified layout requiring less masking. In the summer of 1950, a welcome livery variation was applied to

a batch of 36 Weymann RTs (Nos 3224-3259), which carried Green Line markings, raised 'bull's-eye' motifs between the decks and a pale green central waist band. Following Green Line tradition, they were fitted with yellow and green blinds and carried no advertisements. Allocated to Romford for the busy routes into Aldgate formerly operated by wartime utility Daimlers, they looked magnificent.

Another event took place in 1950, resulting in a more fundamental livery variation involving red and cream, but this had nothing to do with London, except that LT's permission was required for use of the body design. AEC and Park Royal obtained an order for 15 RTs from St Helens Corporation, followed by another 25 in 1952. The RTs looked strange with their 'BDJ' registration letters and the operator's peculiar use of the destination and route number displays. These 40 buses and a single Metro-Cammell-bodied RT which was delivered to Coventry Corporation in 1951 were the only postwar RT family vehicles of LT design to be built for anyone other than LT.

RT4272 entered service at Sutton garage in May 1953 just as Britain was preparing for the Coronation of HM Queen Elizabeth II on 2 June. With posters starting to dull its shining paintwork, RT4272 waits at the bus stand in much-bedecked Epsom. *Geoff Rixon*

Green Line services were particularly busy over the Coronation period and many Country Area RTs were drafted in to help. Crawley's RT3676 picks up passengers in its home town at the start of its journey to the capital. *Geoff Rixon*

This strange contraption consisted of a 1946 RT chassis numbered 0961079 and the body of Tilling ST977. Used for training drivers and engineering staff until its withdrawal in 1954, the vehicle subsequently became RT4761 after a new Weymann body was fitted.
Geoff Rixon

As result of a surplus of green RTs, 13 were loaned to Twickenham garage in March 1954 for a two-month stint. RT4479, carrying a former SRT body, crosses Richmond Bridge on 28 March 1954.
Geoff Rixon

Although there were some exceptions, green RTs were generally built by Weymann rather than Park Royal. Fresh from its first overhaul, RT1092 stands at New Barnet in Coronation year, as proclaimed by the posters on the front of the bus. *Geoff Rixon*

Later in 1950, the contracts with Park Royal and Weymann were renegotiated with a clause requiring a two-year notice of termination on either side. This was unfortunate for LT because an unexpected decline in passenger traffic was just beginning and by 1952 it was clear that too many RTs would be produced. LT gave notice and the final vehicle, RT4794, was delivered by Weymann on 11 November 1954, the numerical last, RT4825, being a Park Royal vehicle which had entered service on 29 March 1954. Between them, the two companies had produced an incredible 5,450 identical RT/RTL bodies for LT, but this achievement was tarnished by the fact that, by the time the last was delivered, the RT was obsolete and its successor, the Routemaster, had already been unveiled to the public. A total of 144 brand-new RTs and RTLs were to gather dust, in store, for several years, the last one (RT4773) not entering service until August 1959.

The Leyland RTs

LT had long-standing links with AEC, going back to the days of the LGOC, and was committed to buying at least 75% of its vehicle chassis from AEC. However, such was LT's desperation to replace its existing fleet, which was either time-expired or non-standard, that it decided to look beyond AEC, Park Royal and Weymann for new RTs, even if this meant sacrificing a certain degree of standardisation and interchangeability.

For running units, LT turned, naturally, to Leyland Motors of Leyland in Lancashire, which had supplied the

◄ Evidence that scruffy RTs were not confined to the 1970s comes from this shot of RTL100 and RT2361 taken outside the Royal Forest Hotel, Chingford, on 7 February 1953. Clearly visible is the difference in the dumb irons which meant that the bottom edge of the cab front swung upwards towards the radiator to enable Park Royal and Weymann RT bodies to fit RTL chassis.
Geoff Rixon

The well-built Metro-Cammell bodies differed from those made by Park Royal and Weymann in several respects, in particular by having a narrower central relief band, weighing an additional quarter of a ton and having different body mountings which precluded interchangeability with other types of body. RTL664, delivered in the earlier livery, lays over at Finsbury Park. *Geoff Rixon*

very successful STDs and Cubs. A total of 1,000 chassis, 7ft 6in wide like the AEC-built RTs, were to be supplied and were to be compatible with the Park Royal and Weymann bodies under construction; additionally, 500 complete buses, with Leyland chassis and bodies, and 6in wider than the RTs, were ordered. The narrow buses, to be known as RTLs, were based on the standard Titan PD2/1 while the 8ft 0in-wide vehicles, to be classified RTW, would be Titan PD2/3s. A number of modifications were necessary to meet LT's specific requirements, including the fitting of the standard preselector gearbox to be supplied by AEC.

Particular problems arose over the bodies to be supplied. In order to relieve pressure on Park Royal and Weymann, LT contracted Metro-Cammell of Birmingham to build the 1,000 RTL bodies, the intention being that these would be of the RT3-type, identical to those produced by the other two builders. However, to accelerate delivery, LT then agreed to Metro-Cammell producing its own design of body to match the others as closely as possible, this body being designated RT7. Metro-Cammell started accumulating large stocks of material and entering into agreements with sub-contractors, only to be asked by LT if reversion to the standard RT3-style bodies could be undertaken. A dispute ensued, which culminated in agreement for Metro-Cammell to produce 450 of its RT7 design of body and, by way of a peace offering, also to build the bodies for the entire fleet of 700 RF single-deckers. LT had been able to reduce its demands on Metro-Cammell for RT-type bodies because it was now 1949, over two years having elapsed since the start of negotiations, and there was a risk of Park Royal and Weymann's output of bodies outstripping the supply of chassis rather than the other way round.

The first RTL chassis was delivered by Leyland in February 1948 and dispatched to Park Royal, where it received the RT3 body originally destined for RT657, whose registration number the RTL also acquired. Of the 1,631 RTLs eventually built, this was the only one to receive a roofbox body from new. The original intention had been for the RTLs to be numbered after the RTW series; thus the prototype became RTL501. Subsequently, the series started with RTL1, but RTL501 retained its original fleet number.

▲ Numerically the first RTL but preceded by roofbox-fitted RTL501, RTL1 waits at Crystal Palace with other members of the class. This bus was one of the first RTLs to be put up for sale by LT and was bought by the Ayrshire co-operative, A1 Service, in 1958. *Geoff Rixon*

RTL400, delivered new to Riverside (Hammersmith) garage in October 1949, stands at Teddington station in original condition. *Geoff Rixon*

Metro-Cammell-bodied RTL583 meets one of Merton's wartime austerity Daimlers at Raynes Park station. The artistic side advertisement has arisen by accident rather than design. *Geoff Rixon*

Another Coronation year view, this time at Piccadilly Circus with the statue of Eros boarded up, finds RTW30 with no ultimate destination. *Geoff Rixon*

RTL501 was sent to Turnham Green on 16 June 1948 to work on route No 91 (and route No 65 on Sundays), introducing the public to its squarer-style radiator and distinctive engine tone, which were the hallmarks of the RTL and RTW classes. Later in 1948, RTL chassis started arriving at Park Royal, just as RT chassis were beginning to run low, and non-roofbox bodies were quickly fitted. RTL1 entered service on 1 December 1948 at Sidcup, operating on route No 21.

The first Metro-Cammell-bodied vehicle was RTL551, which entered service on 24 August 1949. Production continued steadily until the last one, RTL1000, was delivered on 15 March 1951. Although there were many detail differences between the Metro-Cammell and Park Royal/Weymann bodies – sufficient for the bodies not to be

interchangeable with the other types – they looked the same externally except for the pronounced narrower central waist band. The bodies, although a quarter of a ton heavier than the Park Royal bodies, were well made and their added strength was the cause of their remaining in service longer than many of their Park Royal contemporaries. However, no more vehicles of the RT family were bodied by Metro-Cammell apart from the solitary example for Coventry Corporation.

Once the initial order of 550 Park Royal bodies and 450 Metro-Cammell-bodied RTLs had been met, further smaller orders were placed to meet anticipated new vehicle requirements. A total of 631 additional RTLs were built, all bodied by Park Royal except for the last 30 which had Weymann bodies, as did RTL1307. This bus was specially prepared by Weymann to house an exhibition in connection with the celebrated North American tour of 1952.

RTL1631 was the last of the class and the final one to be delivered, arriving on 10 November 1954. Alas, there was no work for 63 of them (RTLs Nos 1568-1631 with the exception of No 1601) and these were stored, along with 81 new green RTs, until they eventually entered service in early 1958. By that time several RTLs had already been put up for sale and one, RTL1222, had been destroyed by fire (at Walworth garage in January 1953). RTL1581 was later to be burnt out at Clay Hall garage (in June 1958).

Unlike the RTs, vehicles of the RTL and RTW classes were exclusively Central Area red buses except for 18 RTLs which were painted green during the autumn of 1959. These operated from Hatfield garage between July 1960 and June 1961, a briefer than expected period due to objections from staff mainly as a result of the RTL's increased vibration as compared with an RT. Apart from RTL501, no RTLs were built with roofbox bodies, but in 1956 RTLs Nos 9 and 36 received RT10 roofbox bodies on overhaul. All three were sold in 1958, but roofbox bodies reappeared on some RTLs in the 1960s as a precursor to the buses being sold, thus ensuring that the more enduring RTs had the later bodies without roofboxes.

Returning to the RTWs, the Leyland body was designed to resemble a wide RT/RTL without a roofbox. The principal

distinguishing feature, apart from the width, was the Leyland-style guttering above the upper-deck emergency exit, although this was subsequently replaced by wrap-around guttering. Another aspect of the emergency exit was the fitting of rubber stops on either side of the rear destination indicator, making it impossible to fix posters in the normal place. Instead, these were placed around the side of the upper deck, adding to the distinctive rear of these buses. The extra 6in width was mainly used to widen the gangways, one of the few redeeming features of the RTW as far as the bus crews were concerned. Like the RTLs, the RTWs were prone to excessive vibration, but more importantly they were particularly heavy on the steering, which made them more tiring to drive.

RTW1 was delivered on 1 March 1949, entering service on 11 May from Tottenham on route No 41. No more than the original order of 500 vehicles were completed, construction ending in December 1950. It had been a struggle for LT to obtain permission to operate 8ft-wide buses even though trolleybuses of this width were operating in east London, albeit the result of a diverted wartime South African order. LT naturally wanted to run the RTWs on the busy central London routes, where the

wider gangway would be particularly useful, but was unable to do so before 1951. Until then, the RTWs were restricted to suburban services, well away from trams and the confined spaces and general congestion of the City and West End. The RTWs were not popular with LT staff, but they worked the normal expected lifespan of some 15 years in public service, so they can hardly be seen as a failure. The RTWs were also invaluable as trainers because their extra width matched that of the Routemasters. Their presence on the streets of central London brought some welcome variety to the constant procession of RTs and RTLs.

The Saunders and Cravens RTs

We have seen how LT's desperation to renew its bus fleet after the end of the war prompted it to look beyond AEC to obtain additional chassis. The same applied to bodies because Park Royal and Weymann were unable to increase production. In addition, therefore, to Metro-Cammell, LT entered into contracts with Saunders of Anglesey and Cravens of Sheffield. Again, the specification was to produce a body as close as possible to the RT3, although it was left to the individual companies to interpret this as they wished.

Saunders received the larger order – for 250 bodies – and set to work designing a product which was in fact very close in outward appearance to the later RT3 (RT10) body. The only obvious difference was that the offside route stencil fitting was not adjacent to the rearmost lower-deck window but was set further back. Also, the bottom edge of the driver's cab front was horizontal since it was not intended that Saunders-built bodies would be fitted on to RTL chassis. However, the body frame itself was very different in construction, with the result that only about 50% of the body contained standard RT parts. Although full standardisation, which LT would have preferred, was therefore not achieved, nevertheless the complete body was interchangeable with those built by Park Royal and Weymann, unlike those built by Metro-Cammell for the RTLs.

The main problem with the Saunders bodies was late delivery. The first, RT1152, was 11 months late and arrived on 22 December 1948, only one month before the last of the 250 should have been delivered. Worse still, there was no sign of any more completed buses. In the meantime, LT found it necessary to hire buses as a stopgap measure. Eventually, Saunders was able to produce a reasonable output and, ironically, was even asked to slow production down in early 1950 because there was a risk of a shortage of chassis. However, by the time the last of the batch, RT1401, was delivered on 1 September 1950, it looked rather archaic compared with the new Park Royal and Weymann buses. This was the result of Saunders' use of the roofbox design and the retention of the obsolete red and cream livery some six months after Park Royal and Weymann had switched to all-over red.

Despite failing to meet delivery schedules, Saunders hoped to obtain orders from LT for at least another 250 bodies. However, LT no longer had the same acute vehicle shortage and considered that its normal two suppliers could adequately meet its requirements. Nevertheless, a token order for 50 additional bodies was given to Saunders and, interestingly, the first of this batch, RT4218, entered service in the same month as RT1401. Saunders was perhaps rather fortunate to receive this further order in view of the previous delays, although it has to be said that the Saunders bodies were well constructed and gave good service, outliving the other roofbox bodies by several years. The last of the second Saunders batch, RT4267, became the final 'top-box' built for London.

Saunders chose to design a body as close as possible to the standard RT body. Cravens, on the other hand, did the opposite, making the most of the freedom to provide a suitably modified standard product to fulfil LT's order for 120 bodies. Externally the Cravens-built RTs looked very different: the side windows were smaller because there was an extra window on each side of the two decks; also the upper deck was more upright at the front end and did not taper sufficiently to line up with the obligatory standard RT cab. In addition, the rear of the upper deck was distinctively curved, so much so that, in contrast with the

RTWs, which, like the Cravens, were fitted with emergency exit 'buffers', it was not possible to affix the normal upper-deck rear advertisements. The interior was also totally different, even to the extent of the window winders. There was no scope for interchanging these bodies with those of other types.

As with Saunders, the Cravens contract was negotiated before LT had decided to discontinue the front roofbox and when LT tried to have the design altered, it was too late, given the size of the orders placed with both companies. Cravens also suffered delivery problems and its first vehicle, RT1402, did not arrive until 22 September 1948. By the end of the year, all 120 should have been delivered, whereas the number was actually two. Matters improved in 1949 and the last, RT1521, entered service in April 1950. Unlike the Saunders-built buses, which were all red, the first 27 Cravens were painted green, thereby breaking Weymann's monopoly of being the sole builder of new Country Area RTs.

The Cravens RTs were a useful stopgap when times were hard, but they had only received one overhaul when LT decided that, in the light of declining passenger numbers and a surfeit of vehicles, the Cravens should be the first postwar RTs to be withdrawn. Besides, they would not fit in with the new overhaul arrangements at Aldenham Bus Works, which relied on a flow-line system requiring a float of interchangeable bodies and chassis.

The first Cravens RTs, all in red livery, were withdrawn on 1 June 1955 when some were barely five years old and by the end of the year only 87 of the original 120 were still in passenger service. No green Cravens had been withdrawn yet apart from RT1420 which lost its roof at Norbiton railway bridge when working a Green Line relief service on 27 July 1955. All remaining red Cravens were withdrawn on 26 April 1956, some having gained a reprieve of a few months through being repainted green around this time. However, even the Country Area vehicles were to go and the last four were withdrawn at Windsor garage on 17 October 1956. All 119 operational vehicles were sold between April 1956 and May 1957 to a dealer, providing a bonanza to provincial operators who were not accustomed

90 TWICKENHAM SUNBURY STAINES

DAZ *boils* WHITEST

DLU 103

SRT128 was one of the second batch of 35 SRTs which utilised earlier STL chassis, in this case from 1937-built STL2104. The vehicle entered service at Twickenham in December 1949 and, ironically, when the SRTs were withdrawn from there in March 1954, they were initially replaced by green ex-SRT-bodied RTs. *Geoff Rixon*

This was the Cravens RT best known to the author in his childhood, because, from 1956, it was a common sight in the Hanger Lane area painted dark blue and used for staff transport by Permutit. RT1487 was in fact one of only two out of the entire class – 119 vehicles excluding the badly damaged RT1420 – not sold to a PSV operator, the other being the now preserved RT1499. *Geoff Rixon*

This view of RT1493 in York Way, King's Cross, shows clearly some of the fundamental differences between the Cravens RTs and the rest of the class: the extra side windows, the flatter, upright front, the pronounced curve of the upper deck at the back and the ill-fitting join above the offside cab window, to name but a few. *Geoff Rixon*

to finding relatively new buses of such quality on the secondhand market at a favourable price.

Many of the Cravens were still running well into the late 1960s, and in a few cases into the early 1970s. The chassis of RT1420 can be found beneath preserved RT1 and some complete vehicles have also been preserved. One of these, RT1499, had the distinction of being hired to LT for training duties in 1978 along with other privately-owned vehicles.

The SRTs

If the decision to order the highly non-standard Cravens-built RTs was questionable, at least the buses had economic value on disposal and they performed satisfactorily in service. The same cannot be said for the SRT class.

Mindful that the imbalance, whereby the delivery of chassis outstripped the supply of bodies, was likely to be reversed by 1949 once the additional body manufacturers had been brought on board, LT considered various options for dealing with the projected surplus of RT bodies. The chosen course was to convert existing STL chassis to take

the new bodies, not as a means of storing them, but to operate as such in public service.

The plan was for 200 conversions to take place using Park Royal bodies and the first batch would use chassis from the STL2516-2647 series. These vehicles, dating from 1939, would be losing their bodies anyway to replace corroded bodies in the 1937-built STL2014-2188 series. Considerable modification would be necessary to enable the STL chassis to accept the new RT bodies, including the removal of the rear section, given that the platform end of the RT body was self-supporting. New RT-style radiators were required but otherwise the main mechanical parts

belonging to the STLs, including the engine, gearbox and brakes, were retained. A chassis production line was set up at Aldenham Works and once the running unit was operational, it was driven to Park Royal for the body to be fitted.

The designation 'SRT' was chosen to represent the combination of STL and RT. SRT1 was delivered on 3 February 1949 and in April the first members of the class entered service from Camberwell and Palmers Green garages. They naturally sounded completely different from normal RTs, but looked identical apart from their old registration numbers and front-wheel hub caps.

Unfortunately, the much heralded 'new' vehicles were derided by their drivers. The engines were sluggish and the brakes inefficient. The cause was plain to see: the STL's mechanical systems were designed to move and stop a lighter vehicle, rather than one which was almost half a ton heavier. Various modifications to the brakes were made to make the buses safer but nothing could be done about the underpowered engines. Drivers preferred to return to the STLs, and SRTs began to be relegated to peak hour journeys. In an attempt to stave off complaints, LT adopted a policy of allocating these buses to less busy routes with no steep hills. The problem was not only with their ability to climb hills when heavily laden, but also to stop on the descent.

LT persevered for a time with the production of SRTs despite the difficulties in their operation and their continued unpopularity. Once SRT125 was constructed, the 1939 batch of the STL chassis with 'FJJ' and 'FXT' registration letters had been used up (apart from six chassis which were deemed unsuitable); LT then resorted to older STL chassis which were easily identified by their earlier registration letters ('DGX', 'DLU', 'DYL', 'EGO' and 'ELP'). The construction programme came to a premature end with SRT160, which entered service on 12 January 1950, but LT was determined that this class should have a reasonable lifespan since it viewed them as largely new buses. However, LT eventually bowed to staff pressure in July 1951, agreeing to the withdrawal of the SRTs immediately after all earlier types had been replaced. An overhaul programme was put in place in 1952, with the vehicles emerging in the new all-red livery and, except for the first two, with full destination blinds. But the programme ended abruptly in May 1953 after 48 SRTs had been overhauled, signifying that the end was nigh. SRT68 was withdrawn on 22 July 1953 and the remainder followed over the next 12 months, the final dozen being taken out of service at Camberwell, Forest Gate and North Street (Romford) on 31 July 1954.

The bodies were quickly removed and fitted to 160 new chassis which had been additionally ordered from AEC, becoming RTs Nos 4397-4556. Not surprisingly, there were no prospective purchasers for the chassis and these were broken up, although 15 received a short reprieve as storage beds for new RT 'float' bodies. Additionally, the chassis of SRT45 saw further service when RT1's body was fitted to it in October 1954, becoming a mobile instruction unit (No 1019J) in the service fleet. But even this was shortlived because, following RT1420's accident in July 1955, the latter's more modern chassis was united with RT1's body to create No 1037J.

The SRT class turned out to be more trouble than it was worth and achieved very little in terms of replacing older buses, bearing in mind the significant cost of modifying the chassis. LT might just as well have kept an extra 160 STLs going, particularly since the last of the prewar STLs actually outlived the SRTs, albeit only by a month. Furthermore, the last 14 ex-SRTs, which became RTs Nos 4543-4556, were surplus to requirements and were put in store for almost a year, entering service in May 1955. Aldenham could boast many fine achievements over the years, but the SRT was certainly not one of them.

Postscript

It would be unworthy to end this chapter covering the production of the RT family on a downbeat note. The failures were confined to the SRTs, RTC1 and, arguably, the Cravens-built vehicles – 281 vehicles out of a total of 6,956 vehicles of the RT family built for London. The RT bus was London Transport's salvation at the time of its greatest need – economical, reliable and popular with staff. It replaced all the prewar, wartime and non-standard postwar double-deck buses (with the exception of the Lowbridge RLHs), the trams (those that survived into the postwar years) and the trolleybuses covered by the first three stages of the conversion programme. It completely dominated London's Central and Country areas from the start of the 1950s through to the mid-1960s and even at the end of that decade still outnumbered the second largest class, the Routemaster.

In the next chapter, which follows the colour section, the remarkably long and drawn-out demise of the RT family in London is reviewed.

This very rare colour transparency taken at the beginning of World War 2 depicts the cinema facing Richmond Bridge. By chance, a prewar RT on Route 37 has crept into the photograph. The vehicle carries wartime white markings on its front mudguards but has yet to be fitted with a proper offside headlight or reduced destination blind displays and window anti-splinter mesh. *Mike Burgess Collection*

To satisfy the need for double-deckers on its busier Green Line coach services, but having rejected the idea of commissioning specially built vehicles, LT decided to use standard RTs. A batch of 36 new green buses, RTs Nos 3224-3259, received a pale green central relief band instead of the normal cream, and Green Line fleetnames. Following tradition, no posters were carried and to emphasise the point, raised motifs were fitted to the outside panels between the decks. The vehicles in question entered service at Romford on 1 August 1950, replacing Daimlers and STLs. RT3233 is seen shortly after its introduction to service on route No 722. *C. Carter*

Hertford's RT93, pictured here on route No 327, was one of seven prewar RTs to remain in passenger service for an extra two years, until 1 September 1957, due to a weak bridge at Broxbourne. *Author's Collection*

Following withdrawal from passenger service, prewar RTs were a familiar sight on training duties for many years. Here, RT101 is parked in front of RTL122 on a wet day at London Bridge. *Author's Collection*

Here is a bus heading for a trolleybus depot on a route with less than two months to run. RTL629 stands at Borehamwood on 4 November 1961. *Gerald Mead* ▶

RT4089 entered service with a Weymann non-roofbox body in May 1951 but is seen here at Waterloo on 25 August 1962 with an earlier RT3 body. The bus carries an offside route numberplate but not for much longer, as 12 months later a start was made on phasing these out. *Gerald Mead* ▶▶

New nearside direction arrows were fitted to the rear of RTs in the mid-1960s, replacing the combined arrows on the offside which were thought to confuse motorists. RT3325 displays the new arrangement in June 1964 while working the short-lived route No 65A along Petersham Road at Richmond. *Mike Harries*

Most sales of RT family vehicles to home customers were made through dealers rather than directly by LT. One of the early exceptions was this example, RT530, which was purchased by C. J. Smith & Sons Ltd of March, Cambridgeshire, trading as Blue Bell. Used on the company's Wisbech service, this bus replaced prewar RT140. *Mike Lloyd*

John Stevenson & Sons of Spath, Uttoxeter, had a collection of secondhand RTs, RTLs and an RTW and was one of many operators to modernise their vehicles by removing roofboxes and fitting platform doors. RT216 is seen in July 1965 wearing its owner's distinctive yellow and black livery. *Mike Lloyd*

During the purge of the RT and RTL classes in the early 1960s, the 500-strong RTW class remained intact. But, in the end, the RTWs became extinct in London first and their demise was swift. Route No 74 received RMs in November 1965 and three months earlier RTW13 is seen at Camden Town. This year was also the period when the cream central relief band on red buses began to give way to mist grey. *Geoff Rixon*

Loans between the Central and Country areas were quite frequent in the 1950s, but were decreasing in the 1960s when Northfleet borrowed some red RTs. Newly painted RT3048 is seen at King's Farm Estate, Gravesend. *Gerald Mead*

Garelochhead Coach Services Ltd was a Scottish purchaser of five Cravens RTs and proceeded to buy standard RTs when these became available in 1958. Despite its relatively high number, RT3662 has an early RT3 body with the roofbox removed by the new owner. The RT was owned by Garelochhead from 1964 until 1971 and this view in Helensburgh shows the vehicle without the owner's name painted above the lower deck windows and displaying an incorrectly spelt destination. *Malcolm King Collection*

◀◀ The last RTWs were taken out of London passenger service on 14 May 1966 and the majority of those not dispatched to Ceylon (now Sri Lanka) were retained for training duties. Harrow Weald trainer, RTW123, negotiates the Marble Arch roundabout in the summer of 1965. *Geoff Rixon*

◀ The first 50 standard postwar RTs were put up for sale in January 1958 along with 50 RTLs. Bradford Corporation bought the largest number, taking 25 RTs, some of which lasted until 1969. No 425, formerly RT411 and now devoid of roofbox, was photographed at Thornaby Drive, Bradford, on 28 May 1966. *Malcolm King Collection*

A total of 23 RTLs received RT roofbox bodies in 1964 as a precursor to their withdrawal over the next three years. One such vehicle was Walworth's RTL73, which was caught on film at Elephant & Castle on 18 August 1966. *Gerald Mead*

◄ Upminster station on 20 August 1966 is host to one of the most famous members of the RT family, the rides bus on the 12,000-mile tour of North America in 1952. The body retained its distinctive roof ventilators when its identity changed from RT2776 to RT1708 on final overhaul in January 1969 – an unnecessary aberration which doubtless contributed to its eventual scrapping in 1974. *Gerald Mead*

Among the purchasers of the first batch of RTLs put up for sale in 1958 was A. & C. McLennan of Spittalfield, Perthshire, which bought five, adding a further four in 1963. A further two were acquired from Dunoon Motor Services in 1964, including RTL1065 seen here in a Perth car park in the summer of 1966. The bus lasted until 1972. *Roy Hobbs*

RT157, formerly with Brown's Blue Coaches Ltd of Markfield, Leicestershire, until this company was absorbed by Midland Red in 1963, could not have travelled much further northwards from its original London home when it was sold again, this time to Simpsons of Rosehearty. This photograph of Fraserburgh bus station was taken immediately prior to the company's absorption by Alexander Northern, whose 1949-built Massey-bodied AEC Regent on the left still exists today. *Mike Lloyd*

With its set back offside route number holder, Wood Green's RT1581 is unmistakably a Saunders-bodied vehicle and is pictured at Northumberland Park on 10 September 1966. *Gerald Mead*

The A1 consortium of independent operators based in Ayrshire, Scotland, operated over 60 RT family vehicles over the years, starting with 25 Cravens RTs in 1956. RTL29 and former roofbox RT4258 display the slight variations in livery adopted by the various owners in this view at Parkhouse Stance, Ardrossan. The RT lasted only three years with its owner, J. C. Stewart of Stevenston, before being broken up in 1966, while the RTL served McKinnon of Kilmarnock for nine years until being scrapped in 1967. *Malcolm King Collection*

The initial batch of 36 Green Line RTs was augmented in 1954 by a further 21 carrying former SRT bodies and numbered RT4489-4509. In 1960 another 28 RTs were added to the Green Line fleet, distinguishable from the original vehicles by having a transfer instead of a raised motif between the decks. The introduction of the RM coaches in 1965 saw the demotion of 62 of the RTs to bus work. RT979 was one of the 23 survivors and still looks resplendent on Derby Day in 1967 as it works the special No 406F service from Epsom station. *Roy Hobbs*

By the summer of 1967, when this view of RTL382 was taken in Buckingham Palace Road, RTLs were disappearing fast from the streets of London and 30 November 1968 saw their final withdrawal.
Roy Hobbs

A substantial fleet of RTs and RTLs was amassed by the Leeds independent, Samuel Ledgard, the executors of whose estate ran the business after the proprietor's death until selling out to West Yorkshire in 1967. RT3622, another former roofbox vehicle, hurries along Woodall Lane on the outskirts of Leeds on 7 October 1967.
Malcolm King Collection

When St Helens Corporation retired its 40-strong fleet of unique London-style provincial RTs, almost half of the class were snapped up by another municipal operator, Kingston upon Hull Corporation. Former St Helens No D25, renumbered 139 by its new owner, enters Ferensway coach station in Hull on 30 June 1968. *Malcolm King Collection*

The first step towards total One-Person Operation in the Country Area was taken on 30 November 1968 when RTs were displaced on the Reigate-Redhill local service (No 430) by 'Autofare'-fitted Merlin single-deckers. RT3203 climbs up Park Lane East, Reigate, during the summer of 1968. *Roy Hobbs*

RTL1023, along with RTL1050, made several trips around Europe in the latter part of the 1960s when owned by Pioneer Coaches (Continental Pioneer) of Richmond, Surrey, and used by the associated Double Decker Club. The company also operated LT's shortest route, the No 235 service between Richmond station and Richmond Hill, after this was withdrawn by LT in the wake of the drivers' overtime ban in early 1966. In August 1968, RTL1023 took 40 passengers and camping gear for a three-week holiday to Estartit in Northern Spain, carefully negotiating several bridges, such as this one, on its journey through France. *Author*

In the late 1950s, the stretch of road between Bishop Auckland and Evenswood in County Durham produced the remarkable sight of four differently liveried RTLs in operation. These were owned by Stephensons, Andersons, OK Motor Services and Lockeys. The last-mentioned's RTL55, seen here at West Auckland on 8 June 1969, was purchased in 1958 and gave its new owner 16 years of faithful service.
Fred Richards

Another small independent operator which ran RT-family vehicles into the 1970s was Charlton-on-Otmoor Services, whose RT398 was photographed at Gloucester Green, Oxford, bus station. *Mike Lloyd*

Lower case lettering on 'via' blinds was introduced in 1961, supposedly as an aid to clarity. By 1969, it was rare to find buses still using upper case lettering, but Catford's RT950, shown here at Bromley North, was one of the exceptions.
Dave Brown

◄◄ LT usually kept its Country Area RTs in excellent external condition, touching-up those areas where the green paint had faded more quickly. The inevitable slight difference in shade is evident here on RT4748 as it pauses outside the former East Surrey Bus Co's offices at Reigate in August 1969. The vehicle has acquired a blue Central Area radiator badge. *Mike Harries*

◄ RT1123 from Stockwell garage ('SW') passes the National Gallery in Trafalgar Square during October 1969. The painting on of garage codes had become standard practice following the discontinuation of stencil plates in 1961, although these were still occasionally used through to the early 1970s in the Country Area on temporary transfers or new arrivals. *Mike Harries*

In the initial period of London Country ownership, the outward appearance of many RTs deteriorated, as evidenced in this shot of RT2935 hurrying past Dorking station in July 1970. The vehicle, which carries the original gold fleetname, will lose its rear wheel discs as its new operator follows LT's example of removing these from November 1971.
Mike Harries

RT operation from Sidcup garage officially ended on 20 May 1977 but route No 51 succumbed to RM operation on 12 June 1976. RT3411 catches the sunlight at Plumstead Common on a Sunday extension service to Hayes station on 25 May 1975.
Michael Furnell

The RT's Indian summer in the mid-1970s brought back the splendour of newly-painted RTs running for a short time with no advertisements in a re-creation of their appearance on entry into service some 25 years earlier. RT436, numerically a very early example dating from 1947, is seen pulling out from Station Approach, New Barnet, on one of the routes which retained RT operation into 1978.
Dave Brown

In this view, taken on 27 October 1975 near Spellbrook, RT1827 carries the Lincoln green and canary yellow livery with the 'circle and bars' symbol on the staircase panel introduced in August 1970 and outlawed by London Country's masters, the National Bus Company, in 1972. The display of the LT 'bull's eye' on the radiator is further evidence of lack of enthusiasm for this unfortunate corporate branding policy.
Michael Furnell

The last London garage to use RTs in passenger service was Barking, where this impressive line-up was pictured. In the familiar scruffy state associated with the final survivors are RTs No 1782, 1561, 2061, 2758, 3342, 2797, 1881, 1088, 2212 and 3754, although none of these actually lasted to the end. *Dave Edwards*

Route No 205 had less than two weeks to run when Enfield's RT953 was pictured at historic Waltham Abbey on 28 March 1976. This loss of RT operation was, however, partly compensated for by the introduction of the No 217B service, the last new RT route on which the class lasted until 20 August 1977. *Peter Plummer*

The Daimler Fleetline was the second generation of RT replacement, but, whereas other operators had some success with LT's cast-offs, LT itself seemed unable to make them work and some ended up in the scrapyard at the same time as the last RTs. DMS2386 and RT2484 stand together at the former trolleybus depot at Bexleyheath. *Mike Pope*

The last Green Line RTs were officially regraded as buses from 19 November 1969, but the type still turned up occasionally on relief Green Line workings in the early 1970s, with Tring garage giving the RT a final fling on route No 706 in 1976/7. If ever there was a testimonial to the reliability of the RT this must be it: a journey through central London from Aylesbury to Chelsham and back in a vehicle some 25 years old (albeit some RFs were emulating this feat). All credit to RT3530 as it basks in the evening sunlight outside Two Waters (Hemel Hempstead) garage on 19 August 1976. *Peter Plummer*

Another RT surprise occurred on 29 November 1976 when Leyton's route No 230, never previously operated by RTs, was converted from RM to RT operation for ten months. RT3230 displays the restricted 'via' blind aperture applied to most borrowed RTs as it picks up at Leyton on 5 February 1977. *Peter Plummer*

Eight years after 'Autofare' Merlin single-deckers took over Windsor's route No 484, RTs still turned up on that service. Here is RT1009 at Langley on 2 March 1977. Sadly, its Certificate of Fitness expired five days later and it was withdrawn. *Peter Plummer*

Although NBC's leaf green livery was much derided, it was the only significant departure from LT red or Lincoln green that any London RTs experienced during their 40 years of service and they wore it well. One of the repainted trio, RT3461, leaves West Croydon bus station in June 1977. *Author*

Route No 26, introduced in its then current form in June 1970, never had RTs until two were borrowed by Finchley garage from August 1976 to November 1977. Newly repainted RT2143 stands proudly at Golders Green. *Dave Brown*

Right through to 9 July 1978, Sunday afternoons would produce the stirring sight of four RT journeys on the M4 Airport Spur (two in each direction) as a result of the No 140 service being diverted to serve Cherry Lane cemetery. In the summer of 1976, RT4559 enjoys this opportunity for sustained running at full throttle. *Author*

Private preservation of RT family vehicles gained considerable momentum in the 1970s and the 1977 Hillingdon Show produced an impressive line-up of 14 postwar examples. Of particular note is the second vehicle, RT1702, one of four Festival of Britain RTs which undertook the first overseas tour in 1950. Note also at the end of the line the only working RT on display – Chelsham garage's newly recertified and repainted RT604. *Author*

RT4721's suspension takes a hammering as the old workhorse pulls out of Heathrow Airport's bus station with a heavy load on 11 March 1978, seven weeks before RMs took over operation of route No 105. *Geoff Rixon*

Bromley garage required only three RTs for its No 146 service; this was an amazing rural backwater for red RTs which lasted until 22 April 1978. RT785 saunters through the byways of Kent shortly before the arrival of One-Person Operated BLs. *Dave Brown*

The last scheduled RT operations into central London were Barking garage's night services, Nos N95 and N98, which were converted to crew-operated DMS operation on the night of 26/27 May 1978. On one of the last RT workings, RT3951 stands outside Broad Street station at 01.40 on 21 May 1978 in preparation for its journey to Romford. *Peter Plummer*

Never had the training fleet received so much attention from enthusiasts than in 1978 when LT's shortage of serviceable vehicles prompted it to borrow privately-owned RTs and RTLs for just over six months. One of the most interesting vehicles to pass regularly through the gates of Chiswick Works that year was Cravens-bodied RT1499, sold by LT in 1956 to the London Brick Co. It was used by the purchaser until 1971 for staff transport. *Author*

During the 1970s, 13 RTs and RTLs were sold to the Sentosa Development Corporation to take tourists around the 700-acre holiday island off Singapore. This view, dating from the summer of 1978, depicts the only roofbox vehicle, RTL247; this vehicle had originally been sold to Doughty of King's Lynn in 1968. During the 1980s, the buses were withdrawn and those that were not broken up are apparently now used as fish farms beneath the sea. *John May*

The third from last RT route was the No 94 service, which was operated jointly by Bromley and Catford garages. This route was finally converted to RM operation on 26 August 1978. Up until then, RTs could be seen on other services operated by these garages, particularly routes Nos 47 and 119A. With just one week to go, RT786 enters West Croydon bus station on 19 August 1978. *Geoff Rixon*

Lesney's, the maker of Matchbox toys, had a large fleet of RTs for staff transport. These were a familiar sight in east London and on the Southend arterial road for many years. Originally painted a dismal dark blue, the buses later became more colourful as this October 1982 shot of RTs Nos 2043, 4399 and 3024 demonstrates. *Geoff Rixon*

Destined to be one of the final dozen to remain in service through to 7 April 1979, RT1798 looks forlorn as it crosses the snowy landscape near Hainault on New Year's Day 1979 on LT's last RT-operated service, route No 62. The canopy number box suggests a previous journey on route No 87. *Author*

The last roofbox RT in LT stock, mechanical training unit RT3062, languished at the back of Stamford Brook garage for many years before being resurrected by Ensignbus of Purfleet in the mid-1980s. That company had successfully tendered for route No 62 and went on to use RTs occasionally on the service until it lost the contract in January 1992. Here, RT3062 turns the clock back eight years at the Gascoigne Estate. The vehicle is now with Blue Triangle. *Author's Collection*

Blue Triangle also owns RT2799, which looks magnificent in this view at Dunmow Post Office on 22 May 1988, when the company operated route No 622 from Great Yeldham Green to Harlow. *Author's Collection*

Of the dwindling number of RT family vehicles still operating abroad, the smartest and most original are probably the six RTs and two RTLs owned by Abegweit Sightseeing Tours on Prince Edward Island in Canada which are allowed to carry their British registration plates at the front. In 1992 RTs Nos 714, 4424, 4188 and 2129 load-up at Charlottetown University. *Trevor Muir*

THE DEMISE OF THE RT IN LONDON

We have seen in the previous chapter that the combination of a reduction in passengers and the requirement to give two years' notice of termination of the RT building contract left LT with surplus new RTs in 1954. It made sense to use these buses to replace the prewar RTs, which were by now showing their age, and the non-standard Cravens-built buses, which had a good resale value.

However, at the end of 1957 there were still 121 brand-new RTs and RTLs in store and no prospect of finding new work for them. LT therefore decided to use them instead to replace the earliest postwar RTs, mainly roofbox-fitted RT3s, and Park Royal-bodied RTLs. On 1 January 1958, 100 vehicles for the UK market and 80 for Ceylon were withdrawn. Unfortunately, the sales staff selected vehicles on the basis of the lowest numbered without taking into account the Aldenham overhaul process, which mixed up bodies and chassis. Consequently, some buyers found that they had paid for a 10-year-old vehicle and received a four-year-old one instead! LT quickly learnt its lesson from this fiasco and checked the origins of vehicles subsequently put up for sale.

LT may have thought that its surplus bus crisis was solved but had reckoned without the troubles that occurred further into 1958. Falling loadings brought major service cuts in the Central Area on 30 April, resulting in 109 surplus double-deckers. The cuts precipitated a seven-week strike by bus crews, further loss of passengers and another round of service cuts in both the Central and Country areas, resulting in the withdrawal of routes and garage closures. By the end of the year there were a staggering 654 surplus RTs and RTLs. Luckily, with delays in Routemaster deliveries, RTs were required for the first three stages of the trolleybus replacement programme and with other prospective double-deck requirements, including the replacement of all the prewar RTs on staff bus duty, only 366 RTs and RTLs were withdrawn for disposal.

The next major event to affect the RT family was the ending of the trolleybus replacement programme in May 1962 because this meant that Routemasters were now available to replace the AECs and Leylands. First to go were the remaining prewar RTs used as trainers; these duties were assigned to surplus RTLs. Then, in December 1962, the Routemaster take-over began. It had originally been intended to allocate RMs on a garage-by-garage basis, replacing every 10 RTs with nine RMs in view of the latter's additional seating capacity. Edgware and Harrow Weald garages were first in line, but understandably the unions objected to the loss of jobs which would arise and the wholesale conversion of garages did not proceed. Instead RMs replaced RTs on a one-for-one basis, one route at a time. This process continued until the last RMs entered service in early 1968.

The 1960s witnessed the withdrawal of virtually all the RT family variants, leaving just the standard non-roofbox RT and a few Saunders-built 'top-boxes'. One of the driving factors was the installation of heaters, a programme which was to be confined to RT family members with a minimum life expectancy of eight years. On the basis that the roofbox buses were the earliest and the Leylands were not well liked by staff, it was inevitable that these would be withdrawn in preference to non-roofbox RTs. In the light of the Country Area heater programme, red RTs were repainted green to enable the roofbox-fitted RT3s and RT10s to be eliminated, the last Country ones running in service on 31 January 1964. The final Central Area RT3s in passenger service survived until 30 April 1965, but the later red RT10s lasted much longer. Since the next target was the elimination of the Leylands, 23 RT10 bodies were fitted to RTLs and the latter's more modern Park Royal or Weymann bodies (but not the Metro-Cammells) were transferred to RTs. It had been six years since roofbox RTLs had been seen because the three previous examples (Nos 9, 36 and 501) had been sold in 1958.

Exactly 58 years after the RT entered service, RTs reappeared in the London area; the brand-new Dennis Dart provides proof that this is a contemporary shot. RT3871 passes RT3062 at Loughton station when both vehicles were operating Blue Triangle's route No 204 during August 1997. *Geoff Rixon*

▲ LT retained the prewar RTs in best condition for staff buses or learner duties. Hounslow trainer, RT132 with discreet 'L' plate, passes under the wires at Harlesden Jubilee Clock in 1960. *Author*

With these attacks on roofbox RTs and the RTLs, it would be wrong to think that the RTW was surviving unscathed. On the contrary, massive inroads had been made into this class of 500 in 1965, as evidenced by the number to be found on training duties. The end came at Brixton garage on 15 May 1966 when RMs took over route No 95 and RTs the No 109. The last rites were performed over the previous night by RTW467. However, several received repaints for training duties.

The end of Routemaster production did not herald a lull in the RT replacement programme because in its wake followed the 1968 'Reshaping Programme'. The main thrust of the programme was One-Person Operation (OPO), with initial reliance placed on a new generation of Merlin and Swift single-deckers, followed by the Fleetline double-deckers (DMS class). These buses would eventually have a

totally different impact on the RT class than the Reshaping Programme envisaged, but in the early days they swept the RTs and RMs aside. When the programme started on 7 September 1968, 22 new OPO services were introduced in the Central Area and, when the next stage was implemented on 26 October, the RTLs were particularly hard hit. On that date the last roofbox example, Cricklewood's RTL453, was withdrawn. The third stage, which occurred on 30 November 1968, finished off the RTLs in passenger service. Willesden's routes Nos 176 and 226 were last and RTL 543 ran the final scheduled working the previous night.

The only members of the RT family now remaining in passenger service were the RTs themselves and next on the hit list were those which had not received saloon heaters, including the remaining 'top-boxes' (all Saunders-built) apart from one which had received a heater in error. Merlins had also reached the Country Area, where they entered service in November 1968 at High Wycombe, Amersham and Reigate. The displaced RTs, which were fitted with heaters, were painted red and transferred to the Central Area to replace those without heaters. As further red and green RTs became surplus in 1969, a start was made on replacing the last RTL staff buses and RTW trainers.

Another Country Area development, which occurred on 19 November 1969, was the reclassification of the remaining 20 Green Line RTs. There had been 85, but the arrival of the Routemaster Coaches in 1965 caused 62 to receive bus livery and a further three were so treated in 1967. The splendid sight of green RTs with their 'between-decks' 'bull's-eyes' and absence of advertisements would disappear.

The biggest change of all in the history of LT – to be surpassed only by its eventual break-up – occurred on 1 January 1970, when, following the transfer of responsibility for LT to the Greater London Council, the Country Bus & Coach Department was hived off to a new National Bus Company (NBC) subsidiary, London Country Bus Services (LCBS). From then on, the red and green buses (which included the Green Line coaches) would go their separate ways. As far as the division of the RT fleet was concerned, LT ended up with a huge number – 2,861 (2,775 in passenger service) – making the RT still the largest bus class, whilst LCBS received 484. This number was deceptively small, but still meant that the RT was LCBS's single biggest type, constituting a staggering 67% of the double-deck fleet. For both companies, the elimination of these elderly and, in terms of crew operation, uneconomic vehicles was an urgent priority. Nobody in 1970 could possibly have imagined that it would take nine years to achieve this.

LCBS wasted little time in applying the new fleetname, 'London Country', to the side of its RTs and also did its best to remove all traces of the LT 'bull's-eye', including the radiator badges. However, for most of the first year (1970), the 'bull's-eye' could still be seen on the Green Rover advertisements carried by many RTs and a few LT radiator badges survived; strangely, these seemed to be mainly blue Central Area examples. In August 1970, RTs began to receive canary yellow central waist bands, yellow fleetnames and fleet numbers, together with the new LCBS 'flying polo' symbol which was applied to the offside of the staircase panel. In fact, yellow had been introduced by LT on its new green buses back in 1968 and even, experimentally, on RT1616 as early as February 1966. Lincoln green remained the basic colour but in early 1972 a lighter shade of NBC green was introduced, although only one RT (No 3752) ever carried this livery.

LCBS pressed ahead with its plans for the total elimination of conductors and increased its order for OPO single- and double-deck buses. However, it quickly became clear that some RTs would be required for a few more years and so 56 were given complete overhauls and five-year Certificates of Fitness between February 1971 and April 1972. Since LCBS did not yet possess suitable workshop equipment, the RTs were sent to Aldenham for this work. LCBS's RT3752 in fact became the last RT to be overhauled at the famous works when it emerged, in its new shade of green, on 14 April 1972.

In the meantime, replacement of RTs continued through a combination of route conversions to OPO and service cuts. LCBS was even able to sell back 34 RTs with short Certificates of Fitness to LT in September 1972. By the end of the year, fewer than 100 RTs remained in service with LCBS. Something of a lull for the type then occurred. Five were loaned to Alder Valley in Reading during 1973, but generally the fleet soldiered on and it was not until 31 May 1975 that the withdrawal programme was restarted in earnest. Unfortunately for LCBS, this coincided with a shortage of Routemaster parts and major engineering problems for the rest of the fleet as maintenance staff tried to cope with the great variety of types of vehicle, many of which were hopelessly unreliable. Dozens of buses were hired from other operators and RTs were drafted in to help out across the network.

When 1976 began, RT-scheduled operations were confined to Harlow, Leatherhead, Reigate, Stevenage, Luton and Chelsham but by the end of the year only part operation of route No 403 at Chesham remained, although unscheduled operations and loans occurred. Tring borrowed an RT for Green Line relief on route No 706 throughout the summer, substituting it for another through to 28 January 1977. From January to March 1977, RTs even appeared on a new service for the last time – Hertford's route No 316. But time was running out for the class. Although 19 remained operational at the end of 1976, the last vehicles with five-year Certificates of Fitness from Aldenham would be withdrawn by April 1977. This caused a problem for route No 403, which prompted LCBS to hire Leyland Atlanteans from Maidstone Borough Council from March through to October. However, as a safeguard, LCBS took the surprising step of recertifying the best four survivors (RTs Nos 604, 981, 1018 and 3461), repainting all but RT981 in NBC leaf green. This colour scheme had been forced on LCBS back in 1972 but, as far as RTs were concerned, had only been applied to two trainers, RT2230 and RT2367, around the end of 1974.

The repainted trio looked superb and when they made their début between April and June 1977 on the No 403 everyone looked forward to a long Indian summer. Alas for RT enthusiasts, if not LCBS, the company's passenger vehicle problems seemed to subside and RT1018 and

RTL1275, one of 18 redundant red RTLs painted green but still unwanted, operates Welwyn Garden City's town service to Knightsfield via Heronswood Road on 15 October 1960. The green RTLs lasted under a year and then became trainers. *Gerald Mead*

had exceeded their expected 15-year lifespan. The only remaining non-standard RTs in service were the Saunders-built 'top-boxes' and since body spares were becoming unobtainable, these were the next to go, along with the remaining unheated RTs. June 1970 saw their demise except for RT1903, the only Saunders fitted with a heater; this lasted until 13 March 1971, latterly at Battersea garage. The last four RT3 'top-boxes', Nos 323, 329, 332 and 337, which had been used as staff buses, were withdrawn by 1 July 1970 and the last RT10 'top-box', No 1866, also a staff bus, was withdrawn on 1 September 1970. Apart from RT1903, the only roofbox-fitted RTs remaining were Park Royal-bodied RT4325, which was converted to a decimalisation trainer in preparation for the change to the new coinage, and Saunders-built RT3062, which became a mechanical training unit, retaining its RT identity (unlike No 1037J [ex-RT1/RT1420], the other such unit). The same year (1970) also saw the last RTWs – 15 trainers – withdrawn and, on 1 October, the last RTL (No 1232), which had been a staff bus at Abbey Wood.

Despite the proliferation of modern vehicles, LT was beginning to experience maintenance problems with the new buses due to their unreliability in service. The last RTs had been overhauled in 1970 with five-year Certificates of Fitness. It seemed clear by 1972 that the extinction of the RT class would not happen before 1975; consequently, a programme of recertification and repainting of suitable vehicles was undertaken, with the best examples receiving three-year Certificates. It, therefore, came as a surprise to find LT, for the first time in its history (apart from when it had bought out other operators), purchasing a large stock of secondhand vehicles – 34 RTs from LCBS. These were immediately repainted and put into service.

Although the programme of replacing RTs by new OPO buses and Routemasters continued, only 260 RTs were withdrawn in 1973, still leaving 1,097 licensed for passenger service. The withdrawals included trainer RT4325, the last roofbox RT apart from No 1037J and RT3062 in the service fleet. The following year was even quieter for the RTs with the loss of only 120 members. Premature withdrawals of modern vehicles, barely five

RT3461 were transferred to training duties in September 1977, where there was a greater need. Lincoln green RT981, which unlike the other three RTs was allocated to Reigate, worked on routes No 406 and 414 until February 1978, when it also became a trainer. RT604 was left to keep the flag flying and continued working route No 403 and sometimes the No 453, until its engine failed in September 1978. There were rumours that a replacement engine would be fitted but it appears that the only spare engine in stock was fitted instead to the Hemel Hempstead trainer, RT1018, whose previous engine was wrongly diagnosed as being defective. This was all rather sad because RT604 seemed on course to outlive the last LT red RTs in normal passenger service. RT604 waited in vain at Chelsham garage until it was disposed of in July 1979, fortunately being preserved.

Following the Country Area split on 1 January 1970, LT adopted the same policy as LCBS in trying to eliminate conductor operation and phase out the RTs, all of which years old, coupled with delayed deliveries of new buses and continuing maintenance problems made it increasingly obvious that RTs would be required beyond 1975. Recertifications would again be necessary, with three-year 'tickets' and a repaint being provided. The wonderful sight of gleaming RTs in service, often free of advertisements for a few days, was a treat no one had expected to experience again. Even better, as a result of RM shortages, the RTs were beginning to appear on routes which had lost the last of the type years ago or had never had them at all; this became more widespread as 1976 progressed. The loaned RTs could normally be distinguished by their non-standard blinds.

Despite the type springing up all around, the erosion of the fleet was continuing. On 28 February 1976, Seven Kings relinquished its record of being the only remaining garage to have a 100% RT fleet and on the same date scheduled operation of RTs on cross-London routes (excluding the Embankment services) ended when Willesden's allocation for route No 176 was replaced by RMs. The RT recertification/repainting programme ceased in March 1976, but excitement occurred on 10 April 1976 when, for the last time, a new RT service was introduced. This was Enfield's route No 217B, which kept its RTs until 20 August 1977. Equally noteworthy was the wholesale conversion of Leyton's route No 230 from RM to RT operation on 29 November 1976; this lasted until September 1977. This was a remarkable event considering that RTs had never worked the route before. By the end of 1976, there were still 539 RTs in passenger service, operating from 19 garages.

The following year would witness the familiar story of RT replacement, but there still appeared to be a great many around, partly due to the temporary loans continuing. A bright spot occurred on Easter Sunday, 10 April 1977, when the 25 silver RMs, repainted to commemorate HM the Queen's Silver Jubilee, were unveiled to the public. Nothing was more fitting than to have repainted RT1599 lead the procession from Hyde Park to Battersea Park.

Most of the temporary loans continued through the summer of 1977 but ceased by November due to a shortage

of serviceable RTs to operate their scheduled services. Over the two-year period, 1976/7, unscheduled RTs had operated on 35 routes from 17 garages. This indeed had been their Indian summer, but there were still a couple more surprises to come.

In addition to recalling the loaned vehicles, LT tried to overcome the RT shortage by instigating a further short-term recertification programme to deal with 65 of the remaining 400. On 1 January 1978 236 RTs were still required for 16 services working from 11 garages, but as far as LT was concerned they were to be replaced very quickly as the availability of serviceable replacement vehicles was improving. Although, mechanically, the RTs were the most trouble-free type in the bus fleet, it was eight years since their last full overhaul and this was evident from the shabby appearance of many of the survivors. The fact that they could operate reliably despite such apparent neglect was nothing short of remarkable.

The onslaught on the remaining RTs started swiftly in

▲ The proposed replacement of the entire Country Area RT fleet by OPO single-deckers began in November 1968 and route No 468 was converted in June 1972. RT4201, pictured here in Epsom on 4 May 1968, was a 'Loadmeter' bus, hence the cut lower panel in front of the rear-wheel arch. This gave access to equipment which recorded the number of passengers. Nine RTs were so fitted at various times, RT4201 replacing the pilot bus, RT4773, which became the last RT to enter service due to the installa-tion of the 'Loadmeter'.
Gerald Mead

January 1978 and by the time the last two services operating into central London, night bus routes Nos N95 and N98, had been converted on 26 May, the only routes remaining were Nos 140, 94 (with some 47 and 119A workings), 87 and 62. Then, amidst all the gloom, another bright spot emerged. An influx of new and untrained drivers required the provision of additional RTs for learner duties since there were no spare RMs. LT, therefore, took the unique step of hiring up to 16 privately-owned, mainly preserved, RT-family vehicles for varying periods between 4 April and 1 November, bringing 'top-boxes', RTLs and even a Cravens RT back to the streets of London. This was a story even the national press could not resist.

Route Nos 87 and 62, operated by Barking garage, were scheduled to be the last to use RTs and withdrawal was planned for October 1978 with conversion to RM operation. But fate intervened for the final time. Barking's bus crews considered it too risky to drive anything wider than an RT over the narrow bridge at Chadwell Heath station. Therefore, although route No 87 was converted on 28 October (apart from one RT working on Saturdays), the No 62 kept its RTs. Luckily, only 10 were required but time was running short because by the end of the year, with Certificates of Fitness expiring rapidly, there were only 13 serviceable examples left. Meanwhile, no improvements had been made to the railway bridge and LT, as a result, decided to re-route the No 62 to enable the RMs to take over.

The final day of RT operation was tentatively fixed for 31 March 1979, but when it was realised that this would clash with the last day of operation of the famous RF single-deckers, the date was put back to Saturday 7 April. By now only 12 serviceable RTs survived: Nos 624, 1301, 1790, 1798, 1989, 2240, 2541, 2671, 3016, 3251, 3254 and 4633. Two of these (Nos 3251 and 3254) belonged to the batch of 34 purchased from LCBS. RT624, nominally the oldest, worked the last public journey, bringing the 40th year of RT operation to a close at 1.45pm. A cavalcade of six RTs, unofficially augmented by some preserved RTs, then lined up alongside Barking garage for a final run starting at 4pm. They waited, as did the TV cameras, the press and thousands of spectators for the star attraction: the first public appearance of the restored RT1 to lead the procession. The excitement generated by the sight of this magnificent machine as it approached the garage is impossible to convey in words. The fact that No 1037J could have been resurrected so quickly (within about six months) and that it was allowed to carry RT1's original registration number despite the chassis having been originally registered as JXC 183 made its appearance on that day seem all the more remarkable.

Thus the RT era, which for so long seemed everlasting, finally came to a close. A few red and green trainers survived for a little longer before fading away virtually unnoticed. RT1018 was LCBS's last, surviving at Hemel Hempstead, although nominally allocated to Stevenage, until March 1981 when its Certificate of Fitness expired. Although not needed for training duties, the Certificate had enabled RT1018 to operate a private hire duty on its 32nd birthday, 9 November 1980, making it the last RT to run in revenue-earning service. On withdrawal, it was bought by an LCBS employee for preservation. The last red RT in stock, albeit not licensed to carry fare-paying passengers, was the Chiswick skid bus, RT1530. This former decimalisation trainer gave pleasure to hundreds of visitors who were able to travel on its lower deck on free demonstration skid runs during the Chiswick Works Open Day held to commemorate LT's 50th anniversary in 1983. When LT ceased to exist on 29 June 1984, being replaced by London Regional Transport, another skid bus (RT2143) and the radio training vehicle (RT2958) were also in stock. RTs Nos 2143 and 2958 were sold in March and April 1985 respectively, leaving RT1530, by now disused, on the books of the newly formed London Buses Ltd. RTs Nos 4712 and 4825, meanwhile, had been retained in the London Transport Museum collection, the former in operational condition and the latter on static display at Covent Garden.

Thus ended the London Transport RT and LT itself. However, the age of tendered routes and private operations would return RTs, at least occasionally, to the old LT area after a seven-year gap. Another era was to begin in 1986.

THE RT FAMILY OUTSIDE LONDON

The RT, RTL and RTW types were essentially London buses, designed by LT to meet the particular demands of operating in the capital. Immediately after the war, various other operators purchased the RT chassis while the first LT bodies were awaited. A variety of different bodies were fitted, none of which resembled London RTs. It was a different position, however, with St Helens Corporation in Lancashire, which, hitherto, had been reliant on lowbridge double-deckers because several bridges were not quite high enough to accept standard provincial highbridge double-deckers. At 2.5in lower, the RT would provide the benefits of highbridge passenger comfort and still fit under the bridges. So, with LT's permission for use of the body

design, 15 RTs were purchased. Registered BDJ 59-73 (fleet numbers 59-73), these buses were identical to London RTs, even down to the style of indicator layout (although St Helens put it to strange use). The RTs looked superb in their red and cream livery and the operator was so pleased with the buses that it ordered a further 25 in 1952 (registered BDJ 801-825; fleet numbers 1-25). The RTs ran until 1960-2, whereupon virtually half of the class (19) were purchased by Kingston upon Hull Corporation, where they worked for another 10 years.

The only other complete RT-family vehicle supplied new to another operator was Coventry Corporation No 99 (GKV 99) in 1951. This bus carried a Metro-Cammell body (the

St Helens Corporation No D73, seen here in its home town in 1953, was the last of the initial batch of 15, entering service in 1950. On withdrawal in 1962, it became Kingston upon Hull Corporation No 149. *C. Carter*

Despite the blinds fitted to RTL1469, this brand new Dalston bus is not departing Britain but merely taking some Americans for an outing. This atmospheric shot was taken at Gillingham Street (Victoria) garage on 6 March 1954. RT4223, from the second batch of Saunders-bodied vehicles, prepares to operate a more conventional service.
Geoff Rixon

RTWs Nos 421 and 422, the only members of their class to undertake an overseas tour, stand between Chiswick's famous gates on 22 September 1950 prior to setting off for the German Industries Fair. Semaphore trafficators and nearside wing mirrors have been fitted for the occasion. On their return the buses went to Chalk Farm and ultimately ended up in Ceylon.
Ian Allan Library

only RT to do so) on an old 1947 chassis – probably a sample originally provided by AEC to assist the company to design its RTL bodies. Unlike the St Helens vehicles, Coventry's RT differed slightly from the LT version, most notably in its indicator design. It remained in service until December 1964.

Up to the mid-1950s, it was not normally possible to see RT-family buses outside London, apart from the 41 mentioned above, except perhaps on overseas tours. Double-deck buses were still very much a novelty in most countries, even more so in Europe where there was little British influence. The dispatch of red London buses abroad was an opportunity to attract visitors to Britain and to

London. Between 1950 and 1957, 15 RT-family vehicles travelled overseas, receiving commemorative plaques and 'GB' plates; these were usually retained during the vehicle's life. Only three lost their identity as a result of the overhaul process.

The first tour, lasting three months, started on 28 July 1950. This took brand new RTs Nos 1692, 1702, 3070 and 3114 through seven European countries, covering some 4,000 miles to publicise the 1951 Festival of Britain. The large gap in the fleet numbers was due to the first two being Park Royal-bodied and the last two Weymann.

The next tour was the only one to feature RTWs. Starting on 22 September 1950 and lasting a month, RTWs

Nos 421 and 422 went to Berlin for the German Industries Fair. This was the only occasion that RT family members ventured behind the 'Iron Curtain' into Eastern Europe while in LT ownership.

The third tour was the most famous, taking RTs Nos 2775 and 2776 and RTL1307 on a 12,000-mile journey across the USA and Canada. The rides bus, RT2776, was fitted with roof ventilators, which the body carried all its life until being scrapped in 1974. RTL1307 was specially fitted out by Weymann as an information office and exhibition centre and was, in fact, the only Weymann-bodied RTL amongst the first 1,600 of the class. The trip started on 29 February 1952 and lasted nearly six months, the Canadian leg being added whilst the vehicles were in the USA.

The remaining five tours were unexceptional compared with the North American venture. Between 11 June and 7 August 1953, RT3710 and RTL1459 visited Switzerland and then moved on to Sweden. In 1954, brand-new RT4760 travelled to Maastricht in Holland for two weeks in June; this was the only red RT in a batch of 110 green bodies being built at that time by Weymann. Indeed, RT4760 was Weymann's last red example. From 16 May to 8 August 1955, RTL117 visited Arnhem in Holland. Finally, in June 1957, RT2422 went to Leeuwarden in Holland for three weeks, only to be sent abroad again for five weeks later in the year. This trip was to Helsinki in Finland, when the bus was accompanied by RTL1486.

By now the RTs were no longer LT's flagship class and RMs would assume the role of overseas ambassador. The RTs had done a great job for Britain: not only had they travelled long distances but even when they reached the trade fair or promotional event they were usually put to work, giving rides to the local population. It is to their immense credit that the representatives performed faultlessly throughout.

Vehicles of the RT family have on occasion travelled abroad after sale by LT. RT73's adventurous trip to Russia in 1959 has already been mentioned. The film *Summer Holiday* encouraged others to travel abroad in old London buses, but they had to remain red to make any real impact.

◄◄ Another overseas tour bus to be exported to Ceylon was RTL1307, the information office and exhibition centre vehicle used in the famous visit to the USA and Canada. This view shows the RTL being lowered into the hold of the Cunard liner *Parthia* (13,350 tons gross) at Liverpool docks on 3 March 1953. Features to note are the 'GB' plate, the rear lights in the central waist band and the grille where the near-side upper-deck rear poster should be. *Ian Allan Library*

◄ On its return from North America, the rides bus, RT2776, carried the tour crews' families on a private trip through London wearing route No 11 blinds. In this view the distinctive roof ventilators above the front windows are largely obscured by flags, but the lower saloon ventilator is visible along with the numberplates from New York, Ontario and Quebec. The only one of the trio of buses to survive is RT2775, which is preserved at Cobham Bus Museum in Surrey. *Geoff Rixon*

RTL1050, when first in the ownership of Continental Pioneer of Richmond, clung to its red livery for several European tours in the mid-1960s and often became a 'scoop' for the local newspaper or TV reporter, duly posing or performing 'run-pasts' as required. Some of RTL1050's exploits were, however, less welcome (but more fun!), such as its unsolicited visits to the Eiffel Tower and the Carlton Hotel in Cannes during August 1967.

Once LT started to dispose of RT family members, they could turn up just about anywhere in Britain, although Wales was somewhat under-represented. Also, RTWs were rather hard to find for reasons which will become evident shortly. The selling process had started in December 1955 when 17 prewar RTs went to a dealer (North's of Leeds), who resold them all for further use. The largest number went to Smith's of Reading and Progressive of Cambridge, which each took four. The next LT clear-out comprised the 119 Cravens (excluding the seriously damaged RT1420), which were sold to another dealer (Bird's of Stratford-upon-Avon) between April 1956 and May 1957. All found buyers in Britain, particularly in Scotland, with Dundee Corporation taking 30 for tramway replacement and the A1 consortium of private operators at Ardrossan taking 25. A1 would eventually operate over 60 members of the RT family.

Standard RTs and RTLs first came on the market in January 1958 when 50 of each were sold to Bird's. The purchaser who bought most was Bradford City Transport, buying 25, the final four of these 25 lasting until 30 April 1969. After the first 100, there was a continuous stream of RT-family vehicles for sale; these vehicles were of interest to operators of all sizes. Samuel Ledgard's of Leeds had 34 RTs and five RTLs; Bedlington & District in Northumberland purchased 25 RTs (these were mainly ex-LCBS vehicles); Barton bought 23 RTLs and one RTW; Jersey Motor Transport imported 14 RTLs; OK Motor Services of Bishop Auckland acquired, directly or indirectly, 10 RTLs and one RTW; and Walsall Corporation acquired five RTLs. These were some of the principal public transport operators; there were other buyers who wanted the vehicles for miscellaneous commercial use, for example

as staff transport. The largest such operator was Lesney (of Matchbox toys fame).

However, the buyers with by far the largest fleets of ex-LT RT-family vehicles were overseas. The Ceylon Transport Board bought a staggering 1,273 buses between February 1958 and December 1968, comprising 266 RTs, 728 RTLs and 279 RTWs (over half of this class). Included were three of the 'overseas ambassadors', RTL1307 and RTWs Nos 421 and 422. The whole fleet, apart from a few airport buses, were driven into the ground over two decades, creating a sorry spectacle but demonstrating the resilience of these old warhorses.

South Africa was the second largest buyer, with the City Tramways Co Ltd of Cape Town taking 177 vehicles between September 1963 and November 1966, primarily to replace its trolleybus fleet. The total was made up of 71 RTs, 102 RTLs and four RTWs. The Municipality of East London also bought 10 RTs and another was acquired privately. Nine in total are believed to survive today, mostly in various states of disrepair, but interest is reviving and RTL1394 has already been put back on the road.

Many other RT-family members were purchased for use at major tourist attractions abroad, retaining their red livery, but most have been replaced now by Routemasters, leaving the RTs to rot or occasionally to be preserved. There is, of course, a large preservation movement in this country and all the different variants can be seen at shows. Also, thanks to two sympathetic operators near London, Blue Triangle and the former Ensignbus, it has been possible since 1986 to travel occasionally by RT in public service, sometimes over a former RT route. Other opportunities to travel on RTs are available on operating days such as those held at the Cobham Bus Museum in Surrey. Travelling further afield, there are three open-top RTs and one closed RTL operated by Guernseybus, a fleet of eight RT/RTLs on Prince Edward Island in Canada, and, for those wishing to travel at 65mph down a freeway powered by a Cummins engine, Davis in California, USA, has six RTs.

There is nothing, however, quite like an authentically liveried RT running regularly in the old LT area. For this,

Not many provincial operators retained the roof-boxes on their ex-LT RTs, but here are two that went further and actually used the roofboxes. Dundee Corporation No 212 is former Cravens-bodied RT1415 and was photographed in the city in September 1959. This was one of 30 bought as tramway replacement vehicles, augmenting the fleet of 10 postwar STLs purchased in 1955. The other view, taken in Leek on 18 May 1964, depicts RT4420 in the ownership of F. Procter & Son Ltd of Hanley, Stoke-on-Trent. *Geoff Rixon/Gerald Mead*

Between September 1963 and November 1966, the City Tramways Co Ltd of Cape Town, South Africa, and two of its subsidiaries purchased 102 RTLs, 71 RTs and four RTWs. In this shot, an RTL is pictured overtaking an RT3 fitted with a Daimler radiator. *Graham Lunn Collection*

credit is due to London & Country, one of the successor companies to LCBS, which operates Lincoln green RT3775 over part of the old route No 473 between East Grinstead and Kingscote to link up with the Bluebell Railway. The vehicle has occasionally operated on other routes, arousing considerable interest and even some consternation when, for example, it was used on route No 406 to celebrate the 70th anniversary of that service on 1 December 1994. Since it was over 15 years since an open-platform bus had operated this route, it was fascinating to observe the reactions of the passengers, wondering whether they were allowed to board and, in some cases, even having to search for the entrance!

Let us hope that further RTs enter regular service again to keep alive the memories of this faithful maid of all work and classic London bus.

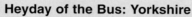
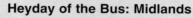